Science in Islam and Classical Modernity

Roshdi Rashed

Al-Furqān Publications: No. 71
Al-Furqān Lecture Series: No. 4

Al-Furqān Islamic Heritage Foundation
Eagle House
High Street
Wimbledon
London SW19 5EF U.K.
Tel: + 44 208 944 1233
Fax: + 44 208 944 1633
E-mail: info@al-furqan.com
http://www.al-furqan.com

ISBN 1 873992 71 8

Al-Furqān Publications: No. 71

Science in Islam and Classical Modernity

Roshdi Rashed

AL-FURQĀN ISLAMIC HERITAGE FOUNDATION

LONDON
(1423 / 2002)

BIOGRAPHICAL NOTE

ROSHDI RASHED is the Director of Research at the Centre National de la Recherche Scientifique (CNRS, Paris); an Honorary Professor at Tokyo University and at the University of Mansurah in Egypt, and the Director of the Centre d'Histoire des Sciences et des Philosophies Arabes et Médiévales (Paris). Since 1977 he has been awarded many national and international honours and medals. The most recent of these (20 September 1999) was 'La Medaille d'Or, Avicenne', awarded to Professor Rashed and his research team by UNESCO.

Professor Rashed is a member of the Board of Experts of al-Furqān Foundation and a member of five Academies. He is the author of numerous works in the history and philosophy of mathematics, number theory, optics, and the history of Arabic sciences and philosophy.

SCIENCE IN ISLAM AND CLASSICAL MODERNITY

Roshdi RASHED

When was the Renaissance?

In 1936, the German philosopher E. Husserl wrote in his familiar style: 'It is well known that during the Renaissance, European humanity underwent a revolutionary turnaround: against the prevailing Middle Ages modes of existence which it now no longer valued, preferring instead a new kind of freedom.'[1] By 'Renaissance' Husserl does not so much refer to the concept used by 15th century Italian literary and humanist circles, nor the concept found later in the writings of Erasmus (where it is related to the renewal of education and religion) as to a concept related to science and philosophy, both closely linked, a concept which would mean more at the end of the 16th and during the 17th centuries. The concept in question therefore appears to be associated with classical science, (that is, early modern science), and makes two claims: it is a weapon of war and a means of

[1] Husserl, *La crise des sciences européenne et la phénoménologie transcendantale*, tr. G. Garnel, Paris, 1976, p. 12.

explanation, or at least of description. As a weapon of war, it was used by both 17th century scientists and philosophers in order to mark a safe distance, real or imaginary, from the Ancients, and in order to promote their own contribution: one only has to think of Bacon, Descartes or Galileo. As a means of description or explanation, the term 'Renaissance' - as made perfectly clear by Husserl - does not explain or describe a completely conventional period here, but just one moment in the intellectual liberation of Europe as it tore itself away from ignorance and superstition.

But Husserl's statement is not at odds with his time: other philosophers and historians believed just as firmly that 'Renaissance', 'Reform' and 'Scientific Revolution' were the most appropriate conceptual terms to describe classical modernity. Almost universally adopted, this view had roots that went back to the 18th century where it was first used to introduce the concept of 'indefinite progress' - as with William Wotton in England and Fontenelle in France. In the 19th century, German Romanticism gave it an anthropological dimension which it had not previously possessed. But regardless of its roots, this belief poses a central question as to the origins and development of classical modernity, which is closely related to science and its philosophy.

Behind the apparent unanimity, this belief had already come under the attack of a fellow scholar of the German philological school, Pierre Duhem. The fact is, his philosophy of science, as well as his religious and political beliefs meant that he, a famous French physicist and historian of Latin medieval science, had a far better grasp of historical continuity and the appeal of the Middle Ages. He therefore dates this classical modernity as far back as the 14th century with the Latins, that is, Merton College, Oxford and Paris University. This thesis has since been contested by historians of ideas and of science such as C.H. Haskins, A. Koyré, G. Sarton, and so on. It has also been contested, but in a different way, in the exceptional works of Anneliese Maier. More recently, Marshall Clagett has attempted to balance the argument. Yet this debate, and the efforts of many scholars during the course of the 20th century, have made it clear that concepts such as 'Renaissance', 'Reform' and 'Scientific Revolution' cannot account for the accumulated facts, and that in the evolution of classical science, the 14th century has been somewhat eclipsed by the 12th and 13th centuries, when the Latins started to make Hellenistic science and Arabic science their own - and this is in fact three centuries before the 'Renaissance'. Traditional methods of dividing political or cultural periods therefore prove inadequate when it is a matter of understanding and analysing classical modernity. Original Islamic works of science are themselves not included here, but they are referred to in their Latin translation, and in this way, maintain a presence in the debate.

Science in Islam

It is this last matter that I should like to take up now - science in Islam (no longer limited to Latin translation alone) and classical science. My aim is to examine how knowledge of Arabic science can bring about a better understanding of classical science both epistemologically and historically. Two features that characterise classical science will be considered:
(1) new mathematical rationality and (2) experiments as a category of proof.

The New Mathematical Rationality

I now turn, not to a philosopher such as Husserl, but to a simple barber, the barber of Baghdad, who expresses himself thus in *The Arabian Nights* [1]:

> *and you find in me the best barber in Baghdad, an experienced doctor, a profound chemist, an astrologer who does not make mistakes, an accomplished grammarian, a perfect rhetorician, a subtle logician, a mathematician accomplished in geometry, in arithmetic, in astronomy and in all the refinements of algebra; a historian who knows the history of all the kingdoms of the Universe. Beyond this, I am in command of all the parts of philosophy; I have in my*

(1) *Les mille et une nuits*, tr. A. Galland, ed. Garnier-Flammarion, [I, p. 426-7].

6

memory all our laws and all our traditions,
I am a poet, an architect . . .

One can see how both mathematics and algebra - in its own right and with all its refinements - occupied a prime position in the encyclopaedia of popular knowledge in the great cities of the time: the barber echoes classifications of far more learned sciences; classifications of, amongst many others, the 10th century philosopher al-Fārābī, or, in the next century Ibn Sīnā, which, unlike other Greek or Hellenistic classifications, welcomed a new independent discipline and gave it its own title: algebra. The popularity of mathematics, its spread and the privileged role of algebra are features of what may be called Arabic science.

Let us briefly go through the genesis of the main features of these Arabic mathematics and, to do so, let us go back to Baghdad in the early part of the 9th century. The process of translation of the great Hellenistic mathematical compositions was at its height and presented two striking characteristics:
(1) Translations were the work of mathematicians, often eminent ones, and were prompted by the most advanced research of the time.
(2) This research was not prompted by theoretical interests alone, but by the needs of a new society in the fields of astronomy, optics, arithmetic, its need for new

measuring instruments, etc. The early 9th century was therefore a great moment of expansion of Hellenistic mathematics in Arabic. And it was at precisely that time and from within the elite circle of the 'House of Wisdom' in Baghdad that Muhammad ibn Mūsā al-Khwārizmī wrote a book on a subject and in a style which were both new. It is in those pages that algebra featured for the first time as a distinct and independent mathematical discipline. The event was crucial and perceived as such by al-Khwārizmī's contemporaries, as much for the style of mathematics as for the ontology of the subject, and, even more, for the wealth of possibilities that it offered from then on. The style is both algorithmic and demonstrative, and already we have here, with this algebra, an indication of the immense potential which would pervade mathematics from the 9th century onwards: the application of mathematical disciplines one to another. In other words, algebra, because of its style and generality of purpose, made these inter-disciplinary applications possible, and they in turn, by virtue of their number and diversity, would, after the 9th century, constantly modify the structure of mathematics. A new mathematical rationality was born, one that we think was to come to characterise classical mathematics, and more generally, classical science.

Al-Khwārizmī's successors began - bit by bit - to apply arithmetic to algebra, and algebra to arithmetic, and both to trigonometry; algebra to Euclid's theory of numbers, algebra to geometry and geometry to algebra. These applications were the founding acts of new disciplines, or at least of new chapters. This is how polynomial algebra came to be; as well as combinatorial analysis, numerical analysis, the numerical resolution of equations, the new theory of numbers and the geometric construction of equations. There were other effects as a result of these multiple applications - such as the separation of integer Diophantine analysis from rational Diophantine analysis, which would eventually have a chapter of its own within algebra under the title of 'indeterminate analysis'.

From the 9th century onwards, therefore, the mathematical landscape was never quite the same: it was transformed, its horizons widened. One first sees the extension of Hellenistic arithmetic and geometry: the theory of conics, the theory of parallels, projective studies, Archimedean methods of measuring surfaces and curved volumes, isoperimetrical problems, geometrical transformations; all these areas became subjects of study for the most prestigious of mathematicians (Thābit ibn Qurra, Ibn Sahl, Ibn al-Haytham, to name but a few) who managed, after in-depth research, to develop them in the same fashion as their predecessors, or by modifying them whenever necessary. At the same time, within the tradition of Hellenistic mathematics, there is seen to be an exploration of non-Hellenistic mathematical areas.

It is this new landscape, with its language, its techniques and its norms, which gradually became the landscape of the Mediterranean. Let us take two examples: rational Diophantine analysis and integer Diophantine analysis.

Rational Diophantine analysis

The emergence of indeterminate analysis - or, as it is called today, Diophantine analysis - as a distinct chapter in the history of algebra, goes back to the successors of al-Khwārizmī, and especially to Abū Kāmil. His book, written around 880, was translated into Latin in the 12th century and into Hebrew in the 15th century in Italy.

Abū Kāmil's purpose in his *Algebra* was to improve upon previous uncoordinated works, and to give a more systematic account; including not only problems and their algorithm solutions, but methods as well. Indeed, Abū Kāmil, towards the end of his *Algebra*, dealt with 38 Diophantine problems of the second degree and the systems of these equations, four systems of indeterminate linear equations, other systems of determinate linear equations, a group of problems centred around arithmetical progression, and a further study of this last group.[1] This collection satisfies the double goal set by Abū Kāmil: to solve indeterminate problems and at the same time to use algebra to solve problems that arithmeticians usually dealt with. In Abū

_____
(1) Istanbul, MS Kara Mustafa Paşa n 379, fol. 79r-110v.

10

Kāmil's *Algebra*, for the first time in history as far as I know, there is an explicit distinction drawn between determinate and indeterminate problems. A study of his 38 Diophantine problems not only reflects this distinction, it also shows that the problems do not succeed each other randomly, but according to an order implicitly indicated by Abū Kāmil. He put the first 25 all into the same group, and gave a necessary and sufficient condition to determine rational positive solutions. Thus for instance

$$x^2 + 5 = y^2.$$

Abū Kāmil reduced the problem to that of dividing a number the sum of two squares into two other squares and solving it. Abū Kāmil's techniques of resolution show that he knew that if one of the variables can be expressed as a rational function of the other or, more generally, if a rational parameterage is possible, then all solutions are possible. Whereas if, on the other hand, the sum has led to an expression with an unresolvable radical, then there is absolutely no solution. In other words, unknown to Abū Kāmil: a second degree curve does not possess a rational point, nor is it bi-rationally equivalent to a straight line.

The second group is made up of 13 problems that are impossible to parameterise rationally. Once more, in a language unknown to Abū Kāmil, they all define curves of genus 1, as for instance the problem

11

$$x^2 + x = y^2,$$

$$x^2 + 1 = z^2,$$

which defines a 'skew quartic' curve of A^3 of genus 1.

Half a century later, al-Karajī, another algebraist, extended rational Diophantine analysis further than ever before. He marks an important point in the history of algebra by formulating the concept of polynome and algebraic calculus of polynomials. In rational Diophantine analysis, al-Karajī differs from his predecessors - from Diophantes to Abū Kāmil - in that he did not give well-ordered lists of problems and their solutions, but instead structured his account on the basis of the number of terms in the algebraic expression, and on the difference between their powers. Al-Karajī considered, for example, successively

$$ax^{2n} \pm bx^{2n-1} = y^2, \qquad ax^{2n} + bx^{2n-2} = y^2,$$
$$ax^2 + bx + c = y^2.$$

This is a principle of organisation which would be borrowed by his successors. Al-Karajī further advanced the task initially undertaken by Abū Kāmil, highlighting - as far as is possible - the methods for each class of problems. We can show the problem which defines a curve of genus 1 in A^3 simply as:

$$x^2 + a = y^2$$

$$x^2 - b = z^2,$$

Al-Karajī's successors have attempted to follow the path that he laid out. I shall not elaborate further on the matter of rational Diophantine analysis in Arabic, and will return to the development of integer Diophantine analysis.

Integer Diophantine Analysis

The 10th century saw for the first time the constitution of integer Diophantine analysis, or new Diophantine analysis, doubtless thanks to algebra, but also, in some ways, despite it. The study of Diophantine problems had been approached on the one hand by demanding integer solutions, and on the other by proceeding according to demonstrations of the type found in Euclid's arithmetical books of *Elements.* It is the specific combination - for the first time in history - of the realm of positive integers (understood as line segments), algebraic techniques and pure Euclidean-style demonstration that permitted the birth of the new Diophantine analysis. The translation of Diophantus's *Arithmetica,* as we know, provided these mathematicians not so much with methods as with problems in the theory of numbers which they found formulated therein. Unlike their Alexandrine predecessor, they wasted no time in systematising and examining these problems: the representation of a number which is the sum of squares, congruent numbers, etc.

This is how 10th century mathematicians such as al-Khāzin studied numerical rectangular triangles and problems of congruent numbers. Al-Khāzin gave the theorem of congruent numbers as follows [1]:

Given a natural integer a *the following conditions are equivalent:*

$1°$ the system $x^2 + a = y^2$

$$x^2 - a = z^2$$

admits a solution;

$2°$ there exist a couple of integers (m, n) such as
$$m^2 + n^2 = x^2,$$
$$2 mn = a;$$

in these conditions, *a* is in the form $4 uv (u^2 - v^2)$.

(1)   R. Rashed, *Entre arithmétique et algèbre: Recherches sur l'histoire des mathématiques arabes*, Paris, 1984, p. 212, English transl. *The Development of Arabic Mathematics: Between Arithmetic and Algebra*, Kluwer, Boston Studies in Philosophy of Science, 1994.

It was also in this tradition that the study of the representation of an integer as the sum of squares started: in fact, al-Khāzin devoted several propositions in his dissertation to this study. These 10th century mathematicians were the first to address the question of impossible problems, such as the first case of Fermat's theorem. But in spite of all their efforts, this problem continued to occupy mathematicians, who later stated the impossibility of the second case, $x^4 + y^4 = z^4$.

Research into integer Diophantine analysis did not die with its initiators after the first half of the 10th century: quite the contrary, their successors carried on, at first in the same spirit. But, towards the end of its evolution, there was a noticeable increase in the use of purely arithmetical means in the study of Diophantine equations [1].

The Tradition Continues

With this example of Diophantine analysis, I wish to illustrate how algebra conceived at the time of al-Khwārizmī was central to the foundation and transformation of this new discipline. As we have seen, the dialectic between algebra and arithmetic has meant that rational Diophantine analysis was considered as part of algebra. And from then on, from al-Karajī to

(1) R. Rashed, "Al-Yazdī et l'équation $\sum_{i=1}^{n} x_i^2 = x^2$", *Historia Scientiarum*, vol. 4-2 (1994), pp. 79-101.

Euler, an important treatise of algebra would always include a chapter on rational Diophantine analysis. This stage marks the birth of integer Diophantine analysis, which would be bound to comply with the exigencies of demonstration. With these disciplines, we have finally seen the rise of elements of a new mathematical rationality which admits the infinity of solutions as a genuine solution. This allows us to differentiate between several types of infinity of solutions - such as the identities and infinitely great numbers - and positively to consider impossibility, or impossible solutions as a subject for construction and demonstration[1]. However, all these features are precisely those of classical Diophantine analysis as it was conceived and practised in the 17th century by Bachet de Méziriac and Fermat. Around 1640, Fermat invented the method of infinite descent[2] which itself would breathe new life into the discipline, but that is another story.

One might ask whether this so-called epistemological continuity corresponds to a particular historical continuity and, if so, to which? To put it more bluntly, was Bachet de Méziriac, at the beginning of the 17th century, created out of nothing? Let us ponder this question for a while, as it effects our subject. My answer would be simply to recall the figure of one of the

(1) R. Rashed, *Entre arithmétique et algèbre*, p. 195 sqq.

(2) J. Itard, *Essais d'histoire des mathématiques* (compiled and translated by R. Rashed), Paris, 1984, pp. 229-34.

most prominent Latin mathematicians of the Middle Ages and the source of many Renaissance writings: Fibonacci, alias Leonardo Pisano.

Fibonacci (who lived from 1170 until after 1240) resided in Bougie and travelled in Syria, Egypt and Sicily, was in touch with Emperor Frederic II and his court. This court included Arabists dealing with Arabic mathematics, like John of Palermo, and Arabic speakers knowledgeable about mathematics, like Théodore of Antioch. Fibonacci wrote a Diophantine analysis, the *Liber Quadratorum*, that historians of mathematics rightly hold to be the most important contribution to the Latin Middle Ages theory of numbers, before Bachet de Méziriac and Fermat's contributions. The purpose of this book, as stated by Fibonacci himself, is to solve this system

$$x^2 + 5 = y^2$$

$$x^2 - 5 = z^2$$

proposed by John of Palermo. This is not just any question of Diophantine analysis, but a problem that crops up as a problem in its own right in the works of al-Karajī and many others. More generally, the main results revealed in the *Liber Quadratorum* are either those obtained by Arabic mathematicians in the 10th and 11th centuries, or are very close to those. Furthermore, the results are placed in an identical mathematical

17

context, namely the theory of Pythagorean triplets, so the conclusion is really nothing new; a prominent historian whose admiration for Fibonacci cannot be doubted had already put it forward. I am referring to Gino Loria who wrote:

> It seems difficult to deny that Leonardo of Pisa (Pisano) has been led to research that had already been summarised by Muḥammad ibn Ḥossein (read al-Khāzin), and his dependence on him is even more in evidence in the following section of the *Liber Quadratorum* which deals with 'congruent numbers'.

We can see therefore that the *Liber Quadratorum* truly belongs to the tradition of 10th century mathematicians, who created integer Diophantine analysis.

Although the case of Fibonacci and Diophantine analysis is not unique, it is exemplary, considering the level it reached. This mathematician, looked at from one direction, can be seen as one of the great figures in Arabic mathematics of the 9th to 11th centuries, but, looked at from another direction, can be seen as a scholar of 15th to 17th century Latin mathematics.

We have seen in this example how classical scientific modernity had its roots in the 9th century, and that it

18

continued to develop until the late 17th century. In this way, rational Diophantine analysis lived on into the 18th century, whereas integer Diophantine analysis underwent a new revolution in the mid-17th century. We also see that this modernity was written about in Arabic in the early stages, that it was then transmitted through Latin, Hebrew and Italian, before going on to become part of significant new research. And finally, we see that the rational core of this modernity was algebra, and that the conditions which allowed it to exist are inherent in the new ontology contained within its discipline.

With this description, we are very far from the prevailing global attitude, and the term 'Renaissance' seems rather an inadequate one to describe the mathematical facts.

Experiments as a Category of Proof

Let us now look at the second feature of classical scientific modernity. I refer here to experimental norms such as norms of proof. To put it briefly, the reduction of the separation between science and art, as well as the change in their relationship in Islamic civilisation - a civilisation which was far more urbanised than previous civilisations - resulted largely in the extension of empirical research, and the genesis of a vague idea of experimentation. Thereafter, the systematic use of empirical procedures increased; for example, in botanical and linguistic classifications, physicians' control experiments and alchemists' experiments, physicians' clinical observations and comparative diagnostics. But it is necessary to wait for the establishment of new relations between mathematics and physics before we see the still unclear notion of experimentation granted the dimension that would define it: systematic and ordered proof. This concept was completely new, and should not be confused with that of controlled, or even measured, observation in astronomy. This time, it will become necessary to take into account the very existential nature of examined phenomena. Optics was the first discipline where such an idea first saw the light of day, before being further worked on in mechanics. The concept emerged for the first time in this form in the works of Ibn al-Haytham, specifically in his book *Optics*, translated into Latin in the 12th century, and later into Italian. Republished by Risner in the 16th century, it was the reference book of all scholars during the Middle Ages, and later for Kepler, Descartes and Malebranche, among many others.[1]

In order to understand the emergence of the new norms and practices, we should briefly recall Ibn al-Haytham's project. He was involved for the greater part of his writings in effecting a programme of reform within the discipline, which was precisely what led him

(1) On the optic works of Ibn al-Haytham, see our *Optique et mathématiques: recherches sur la pensée scientifique en arabe*, Variorum, Aldershot, 1992; and *Géométrie et Dioptrique au Xᵉ siècle. Ibn Sahl, al-Qūhī et Ibn al-Haytham*, Paris, Les Belles-Lettres, 1993. (An English translation of this book will be published by al-Furqan Foundation in 2003).

to revisit the various different disciplines, one by one: optics, meteorological optics, catoptrics, burning mirrors, dioptrics, burning sphere, physical optics. The fundamental act of this reform consisted in clearly distinguishing between conditions for propagation of light and conditions for viewing objects. This reform has, on the one hand, lent physical support to the rules of propagation (in the case of a true mathematical analogy between a mechanical model of the movement of a solid ball thrown against an obstacle, and a similar movement of light) and, on the other hand, led to the use of geometrical procedures and experimentation everywhere. Optics no longer meant what it had meant to the Greeks: that is, a geometry of perception. It now came in two parts: a theory of vision, to which the physiology of the eye and the psychology of perception are also linked; and a theory of light, to which geometrical optics and physical optics are linked. This reform has led to - among other things - the emergence of new questions, never before formulated, for example, examination of the spherical lens and the spherical diopter, not only as burning devices, but also as optical instruments, in dioptrics. It also led to the creation of a new practice of investigation, together with a new lexicon, that of experimentation.

But what does Ibn al-Haytham mean by 'experimentation'? One finds in the works of Ibn al-Haytham as many different meanings of the word, and as many different functions assumed by experimentation as there are relations between mathematics and physics. These relations are effectively established according to various modes. They are not organised around a particular theme by Ibn al-Haytham, but they are implicit in the various works, and it is possible to analyse them.

The reform of geometric optics is Ibn al-Haytham's main contribution to the field: and the unique relationship between mathematics and physics in geometric optics is an isomorphism of structures. But because he had already defined a beam of light, Ibn al-Haytham was able to write about the phenomena of propagation, including the phenomenon of diffusion, in such a way that they perfectly fit the laws of geometry. Several experimental devices were invented as a technical check for propositions whose language had already been controlled by geometry: experiments designed to test the laws and rules of geometrical optics. A reading of the works of Ibn al-Haytham testifies above all to two important facts: first of all, Ibn al-Haytham's experiments were not designed merely to test qualitative assertions, but also to obtain quantitative results, and secondly, the devices conceived by Ibn al-Haytham were varied and complex for their time, and were not limited to those used by astronomers.

In physical optics, there is another type of relationship to be found between mathematics and physics, and later a second meaning of the word 'experimentation'. The contribution of mathematics at this stage is in the analogies between diagrams of the movement of a heavy body and diagrams of reflection and refraction. In other words, mathematics was introduced into physical optics by means of dynamic diagrams of the movement of heavy bodies that were presumed to be already mathematised. It is precisely this preliminary mathematisation of the concepts of physical doctrine that allowed them to be transferred to the level of an experimental situation. Although this was definitely a temporary stage, it nevertheless provided a level of existence for concepts which - although semantically indeterminate - were syntactically structured, such as Ibn al-Haytham's diagram of projectile movement, later taken up by Kepler and Descartes.

A third type of experimentation, not practised by Ibn al-Haytham himself, but made possible by his reforms and discoveries in optics, appeared at the end of the 13th century in the works of his successor al-Fārisī. In this case, the established relationship between mathematics and physics tends towards the construction of a model, then subsequently, through geometry, towards the systematic reduction of the propagation of light in a natural environment to its propagation in a manufactured object: it becomes a matter of defining a truly mathematical analogical correspondence between the natural and the manufactured object, as for example, the model of a massive glass sphere filled with water, to explain the rainbow. Experimentation here has the function of expressing the physical conditions of a phenomenon that could not otherwise be studied either directly or completely.

Other examples could be added to these three types of experimentation, but it is enough to say that - despite the difference in functions they fulfil - the three types of experimentation that we have just studied are all control mechanisms as well as levels of existence for syntactically structured notions. In this they are significantly different from observation - even traditional astronomical observation. In all three types we are in situations where the scientist intends physically to construct the subject himself, in order to be able to think about it: physically realising an idea that could not previously be realised.

Ibn al-Haytham's reforms survived him, as did his establishment of experimental norms as an integral part of a physics proof. From Ibn al-Haytham down through Kepler and other 17th century scientists, the line of descent is established. And a knowledge of Arabic science is necessary for our understanding of classical modernity: it enables us to grasp the introduction of experimental norms, and also to understand better the emergence, in the late 17th century, of a still unknown dimension of experimentation, namely the quest for precision.

Conclusion

To conclude then, let us recall the two central points of this paper. We began by seeing that the new possibilities afforded by algebra were the origin of a new strategy and of a new rationality. This strategy was inherent in algebra's own development after al-Khwārizmī, as well as in its relationship with other mathematical disciplines. It is a strategy that consisted of increasingly exhibiting structures and operations in algebra, and initiating the previously mentioned dialectic of application in its relationship with other disciplines. As far as the new rationality is concerned, it is based on a new ontology of mathematical subjects, making possible what was not possible before. For example, the same subject could be determined both geometrically and arithmetically; a problem could have an infinite number of true solutions; an approximate solution could be a true solution; an impossible solution could also be a true solution; the same procedure could be applied to different objects without additional justification, etc.

We have also witnessed the rise of the new concept of proof in physics, and we have seen how, from then on, it was accepted that the level on which a physical object existed was no longer its 'natural' level, but was within the realms of the experimental.

This new rationality, which can in summary be called algebraic and experimental, characterises classical modernity, and was, as we have said, founded between the 9th and 12th centuries by scholars as far apart as Muslim Spain and China, all of whom were writing in Arabic. Appropriation of this new rationality by scholars began in the 12th century, and a new improved version was to appear from the 16th century onwards. It would therefore seem that whoever wishes to understand classical modernity should not subscribe to the historian's idea of periods or eras, since these are founded on causal links between events of political, religious and literary Renaissance history and events in science: rather, he or she should go in search of true paths, and leave aside the myths and legends which led such great minds as Husserl's astray.

Science en Islam et Modernité Classique

Roshdi Rashed

En 1936, le philosophe allemand E. Husserl écrit dans
le style que l'on sait: "Il est bien connu que l'humanité
européenne accomplit en elle-même à la Renaissance
un retournement révolutionnaire: elle se tourne contre
les modes d'existence qui étaient jusque-là les siens,
ceux du Moyen Âge, elle les déprécie, elle veut se
donner une nouvelle forme de liberté"[1]. Par
"Renaissance", le philosophe désigne ici moins le
concept manié par les milieux littéraires et humanistes
italiens du XVe siècle, ou tel qu'on le rencontre plus
tard dans les écrits d'Érasme, lié au renouvellement de
l'éducation et de la religion; qu'un concept lié à la
science et à la philosophie qui lui est intimement
attachée, c'est-à-dire un concept qui prend son sens à la
fin du XVIe siècle et au XVIIe siècle. Ce concept
apparaît donc ici associé à la science classique, et doté
d'une double prétention: arme de combat, et moyen

---

[1] Husserl, *La crise des sciences européenne et la phénoménologie
transcendantale*, tr. G. Garnel, Paris, 1976, p. 12.

d'explication, ou tout au moins de description. Arme de combat, les savants du XVIIe siècle aussi bien que les philosophes y eurent recours pour marquer leurs distances, réelles ou imaginaires, avec les anciens, et promouvoir leur propre contribution: que l'on pense à Bacon, Descartes ou Galilée. Moyen de description sinon d'explication, le terme de "Renaissance", comme le laisse bien entendre Husserl, n'est pas là pour désigner une périodisation somme toute conventionnelle, mais pour décrire un moment de ce mouvement de libération intellectuelle de l'Europe s'arrachant à l'ignorance et à la superstition.

Mais la déclaration de Husserl n'est pas en discordance avec son époque: d'autres philosophes et historiens croyaient tout aussi fermement que "Renaissance", "Réforme", "Révolution scientifique", sont les instruments les plus aptes à décrire la modernité classique. Presque partout admise, cette opinion s'enracinait pourtant bien loin: au XVIIIe siècle d'abord, où elle servit à introduire la notion de progrès indéfini - comme chez William Wotton en Angleterre et Fontenelle en France; au XIXe siècle ensuite, où elle revêt, avec le Romantisme Allemand, la dimension anthropologique qu'elle ne possédait pas auparavant. Mais, quelles qu'en soient les sources, cette croyance pose la question centrale des origines et du développement de la modernité classique, fondamentalement liée à la science et à sa philosophie.

Mais, derrière cette unanimité apparente, cette croyance était en fait déjà fortement menacée, ébranlée sous les coups d'un homme du même camp, c'est-à-dire lui-même sous l'influence de l'école philologique allemande: Pierre Duhem. Je rappelle pour mémoire qu'en raison de sa philosophie des sciences, mais aussi des options religieuses et politiques qui étaient les siennes, le célèbre physicien français et historien des sciences médiévales, Pierre Duhem, était plus que bien d'autres sensible à une certaine continuité historique, ainsi qu'à l'attrait du Moyen Âge. Aussi fait-il remonter cette modernité classique au XIVᵉ siècle, chez les Latins, c'est-à-dire au Merton College à Oxford et à l'Université de Paris. Cette thèse a ensuite été combattue par des historiens des idées et des sciences comme C. H. Haskins, A. Koyré, G. Sarton, etc. Elle l'a été aussi, mais autrement, dans les travaux exceptionnels d'Anneliese Maier. Plus récemment, Marshall Clagett a tenté d'équilibrer la balance. Mais, de ce débat, et des efforts fournis par bien d'autres savants au cours de ce siècle, il est clairement apparu que des concepts tels que "Renaissance", "Réforme", "Révolution Scientifique", ne peuvent pas rendre compte des faits accumulés; et, dans la formation de la science classique, le XIVᵉ siècle s'est vu quelque peu éclipser par les XII-XIIIᵉ siècles, où les Latins se sont mis à s'approprier la science hellénistique, et la science arabe – c'est-à-dire en fait trois siècles avant la "Renaissance". La périodisation politique ou culturelle des historiens se révèle donc inadéquate lorsqu'il s'agit de la compréhension et de l'analyse de la modernité classique. D'autre part, la science en Islam, absente, au moins en personne, de ce débat, se trouve invoquée au titre des traductions latines faites à partir de ses œuvres. Ainsi, cette grande absente n'a pourtant jamais cessé d'être là.

C'est précisément cette dernière question que je voudrais reprendre ici, c'est-à-dire celle de la science en Islam (non plus limitée à ses seules traductions latines) et de la science classique. Mon but est le suivant: examiner ce que la connaissance de la science arabe peut apporter à une meilleure compréhension à la fois épistémologique et historique de la science classique. Deux traits caractérisent celle-ci, que nous considérerons ici: la nouvelle rationalité mathématique, et la dimension expérimentale comme catégorie de la preuve.

Ce n'est pas un philosophe comme Husserl que j'invoquerai à présent, mais un simple barbier, le barbier de Bagdad qui s'exprime ainsi dans *Les Mille et une Nuits* [1]:

> "[...] et vous avez en ma personne le meilleur barbier de Bagdad, un médecin expérimenté, un chimiste très profond, un astrologue qui ne se trompe point, un grammairien achevé, un parfait rhétoricien, un logicien subtil, un mathématicien accompli dans la géométrie, dans l'arithmétique, dans l'astronomie et dans tous les raffinements de l'algèbre; un historien qui sait l'histoire de

[1] *Les mille et une nuits*, tr. A. Galland, ed. Garnier-Flammarion, [I, p. 426-7].

30

tous les royaumes de l'Univers. Outre cela, je possède toutes les parties de la philosophie; j'ai dans ma mémoire toutes nos lois et toutes nos traditions, je suis poète, architecte [...]".

Non seulement, on le voit bien, les mathématiques occupent une place de choix dans l'Encyclopédie du savoir populaire dans les grandes villes de ce temps, mais l'algèbre y figure "en personne", avec ses raffinements. Or le barbier se fait ici l'écho de classifications des sciences bien plus savantes, celles du philosophe du Xe siècle al-Fārābī, d'Avicenne au siècle suivant, parmi bien d'autres, qui, contrairement à d'autres classifications grecques ou hellénistiques, accueillent une nouvelle discipline, indépendante, et lui confèrent un titre propre: l'algèbre. La popularité des mathématiques, leur diffusion et le rôle privilégié de l'algèbre sont donc des traits de ce que l'on convient d'appeler la science arabe.

Poursuivons brièvement ici la genèse des principaux traits de ces mathématiques arabes. Pour cela, revenons à Bagdad au début du IXe siècle. L'entreprise de traduction des grandes compositions mathématiques hellénistiques est à son apogée, et présente deux caractéristiques frappantes: les traductions sont l'œuvre de mathématiciens, souvent de premier ordre, et elles sont suscitées par la recherche la plus avancée de l'époque. Cette recherche elle-même n'a pas été animée par les seuls intérêts théoriques, mais aussi par les besoins de la nouvelle société, en astronomie, en optique, en arithmétique, dans le domaine des instruments de mesure, etc. Le début du IXe siècle est donc un grand moment d'expansion en arabe des mathématiques hellénistiques. Or c'est précisément à cette période, et dans ce milieu - celui de la "Maison de la Sagesse" à Bagdad - que Muḥammad ibn Mūsā al-Khwārizmī rédige un livre dont le sujet et le style sont nouveaux. C'est dans ces pages en effet que surgit pour la première fois l'algèbre comme discipline mathématique distincte et indépendante. L'événement fut crucial, et perçu comme tel par les contemporains, tant pour le style de cette mathématique que pour l'ontologie de son objet, et, plus encore, la richesse des possibilités qu'elle offrait désormais. Le style est à la fois algorithmique et démonstratif, et, d'ores et déjà, avec cette algèbre, on entrevoit l'immense potentialité qui imprégnera les mathématiques à partir du IXe siècle: l'application des disciplines mathématiques les unes aux autres. En d'autres termes, si l'algèbre, en raison de son style et de la généralité de son objet, a rendu ces applications possibles, celles-ci, par leur nombre et la diversité de leur nature, ne cesseront de modifier la configuration des mathématiques après le IXe siècle. Une nouvelle rationalité mathématique vient ainsi de voir le jour; elle caractérisera, pensons-nous, les mathématiques, et plus généralement la science, classiques.

Les successeurs d'al-Khwārizmī entreprennent progressivement l'application de l'arithmétique à l'algèbre, de l'algèbre à l'arithmétique, de l'une et de l'autre à la trigonométrie, de l'algèbre à la théorie euclidienne des nombres, de l'algèbre à la géométrie, de la géométrie à l'algèbre. Ces applications furent toujours les actes fondateurs de nouvelles disciplines, ou tout au moins de nouveaux chapitres. Ainsi verront le jour l'algèbre des polynômes, l'analyse combinatoire, l'analyse numérique, la résolution numérique des équations, la nouvelle théorie des nombres, la construction géométrique des équations. D'autres effets résulteront de ces multiples applications, comme la séparation de l'analyse diophantienne entière de l'analyse diophantienne rationnelle, devenue un chapitre à part entière de l'algèbre, sous le titre de l'"analyse indéterminée".

A partir du IXe siècle, le paysage mathématique n'est donc plus le même: il se transforme, ses horizons reculent. On assiste tout d'abord à l'extension de l'arithmétique et de la géométrie hellénistiques: théorie des coniques, théorie des parallèles, études projectives, méthodes archimédiennes pour la mesure des aires et des volumes courbes, problèmes isopérimétriques, transformations géométriques: tous ces domaines deviennent objet d'étude pour les mathématiciens les plus prestigieux – Thābit ibn Qurra, al-Qūhī, Ibn Sahl, Ibn al-Haytham, entre autres – qui parviennent, par de profondes recherches, à les développer dans le même style que leurs devanciers, ou en le modifiant lorsque cela s'impose. D'autre part, au sein de ces mathématiques hellénistiques elles-mêmes, on aménage des régions non hellénistiques.

C'est ce paysage nouveau, avec sa langue, ses techniques et ses normes, qui, de proche en proche, deviendra celui de la Méditerranée. Prenons-en deux exemples: l'analyse diophantienne rationnelle et l'analyse diophantienne entière.

L'émergence de l'analyse indéterminée, ou, comme on la nomme aujourd'hui, de l'analyse diophantienne, comme chapitre distinct de l'algèbre, remonte aux successeurs d'al-Khwārizmī, et notamment à Abū Kāmil, dans son livre écrit vers 880, traduit en latin au XIIᵉ siècle, et en hébreu, en Italie, au XVᵉ siècle.

Abū Kāmil entend donc dans son *Algèbre* ne plus s'arrêter à un exposé dispersé, mais donner un exposé plus systématique, où apparaissent, outre les problèmes et les algorithmes de solution, les méthodes. Abū Kāmil, il est vrai, traite dans une dernière partie de son *Algèbre*, de 38 problèmes diophantiens du second degré et des systèmes de ces équations, quatre systèmes d'équations linéaires indéterminées, d'autres systèmes d'équations linéaires déterminées, un ensemble de problèmes qui se ramènent aux progressions arithmétiques, et une étude de celles-ci[1]. Cet ensemble répond au double but fixé par Abū Kāmil: résoudre des problèmes indéterminés, et d'autre part résoudre par l'algèbre des problèmes traités alors par les arithméticiens. Notons que c'est dans l'*Algèbre* d'Abū

_____

(1) Istanbul, MS Kara Mustafa Paşa nº 379, fol. 79r-110v.

34

Kāmil que l'on rencontre pour la première fois dans l'histoire - à ma connaissance - une distinction explicite entre des problèmes déterminés et des problèmes indéterminés. Or l'examen de ces 38 problèmes diophantiens non seulement reflète cette distinction; il montre en outre que ces problèmes ne se succèdent pas au hasard, mais selon un ordre indiqué en filigranne par Abū Kāmil. Les vingt-cinq premiers relèvent ainsi tous d'un seul et même groupe, pour lequel Abū Kāmil donne une condition nécessaire et suffisante pour déterminer les solutions rationnelles positives. Soit par exemple

$$x^2 + 5 = y^2.$$

Abū Kāmil ramène le problème à celui de partager un nombre somme de deux carrés en deux autres carrés, qu'il résout. Les techniques de solution d'Abū Kāmil montrent qu'il sait que, si l'une des variables peut être exprimée comme fonction rationnelle de l'autre, ou, plus généralement, en d'autres termes, si l'on peut avoir un paramétrage rationnel, on a *toutes* les solutions; alors qu'en revanche si la somme nous conduit à une expression dont le radical est incontournable, on n'a aucune solution. En d'autres termes, inconnus d'Abū Kāmil: une courbe du second degré ne possède aucun point rationnel, ou est birationnellement équivalente à une droite.

Le second groupe est constitué de treize problèmes qu'il est impossible de paramétrer rationnellement; ou, cette fois encore dans un langage inconnu d'Abū Kāmil, ils définissent tous des courbes du genre 1, comme par exemple le problème

$$x^2 + x = y^2,$$
$$x^2 + 1 = z^2,$$

qui définit une quartique gauche, courbe de A^3 du genre 1.

Un demi-siècle après, un autre algébriste donne à l'analyse diophantienne rationnelle une extension jamais atteinte auparavant: il s'agit d'al-Karajī. Celui-ci marque un point important en histoire de l'algèbre, en formulant la notion de polynôme et le calcul algébrique sur les polynômes. En analyse diophantienne rationnelle, al-Karajī, à la différence de ses prédécesseurs - de Diophante à Abū Kāmil - ne donne plus de listes ordonnées des problèmes et de leurs solutions, mais il organise son exposé autour du nombre des termes dont se compose l'expression algébrique, et de la différence entre leurs puissances. Il considère par exemple successivement

$$ax^{2n} \pm bx^{2n-1} = y^2, \qquad ax^{2n} + bx^{2n-2} = y^2,$$
$$ax^2 + bx + c = y^2.$$

Ce principe d'organisation sera d'ailleurs emprunté par ses successeurs. D'autre part, il mène plus loin la tâche amorcée par Abū Kāmil, qui consiste à dégager autant que possible les méthodes pour chaque classe de problèmes. Signalons simplement le problème

$$x^2 + a = y^2$$

$$x^2 - b = z^2,$$

qui définit une courbe de genre 1 dans A^3.

Les successeurs d'al-Karajī ont tenté d'avancer sur le chemin par lui tracé; mais je ne m'étendrai pas davantage sur cette question de l'analyse diophantienne rationnelle en arabe, pour revenir au commencement et au développement de l'analyse diophantienne entière.

Au Xe siècle, on assiste pour la première fois à la constitution de l'analyse diophantienne entière, ou nouvelle analyse diophantienne, grâce à l'algèbre sans doute, mais aussi contre elle. On a en effet abordé l'étude des problèmes diophantiens, en exigeant d'une part d'obtenir des solutions entières, et d'autre part de procéder par démonstrations du type de celles d'Euclide dans les livres arithmétiques des *Éléments*. C'est cette combinaison explicite - pour la première fois dans l'histoire - du domaine numérique restreint aux entiers positifs interprétés comme segments de droites, de techniques algébriques, et de l'exigence de démontrer dans le pur style euclidien, qui a permis le commencement de cette nouvelle analyse diophantienne. La traduction des *Arithmétiques* de Diophante a fourni à ces mathématiciens, on le comprendra, moins des méthodes que certains problèmes de théorie des nombres qui s'y trouvaient formulés, et qu'ils n'hésitèrent pas à systématiser et à examiner pour eux-mêmes, contrairement à leur prédécesseur alexandrin. Tels sont par exemple les problèmes de représentation d'un nombre comme somme de carrés, les nombres congruents, etc.

Ainsi, les mathématiciens du Xe siècle, comme al-Khāzin ont étudié les triangles rectangles numériques, et les problèmes des nombres congruents. Al-Khāzin donne le théorème des nombres congruents d'une manière équivalente à celle-ci [1]:

soit a un entier naturel donné, les conditions suivantes sont équivalentes:

    1°   le système

$$x^2 + a = y^2$$

$$x^2 - a = z^2$$

admet une solution;

    2°   il existe un couple d'entiers (m, n) tels que

$$m^2 + n^2 = x^2,$$

$$2\,mn = a;$$

dans ces conditions, a est de la forme $4\,uv\,(u^2 - v^2)$.

The footnote

(1)   R. Rashed, *Entre arithmétique et algèbre: Recherches sur l'histoire des mathématiques arabes*, Paris, 1984, p. 212, English transl. *The Development of Arabic Mathematics: Between Arithmetic and Algebra*, Kluwer, Boston Studies in Philosophy of Science, 1994.

C'est dans cette tradition que l'on a également engagé l'étude de la représentation d'un entier comme somme de carrés. Ainsi, al-Khāzin consacre plusieurs propositions de son mémoire à cette étude. Ce sont également ces mathématiciens qui, les premiers, ont posé la question des problèmes impossibles, tels que le premier cas du théorème de Fermat. Ce problème n'a cessé, malgré tout, de préoccuper les mathématiciens, qui, plus tard, ont énoncé l'impossibilité du second cas, $x^4 + y^4 = z^4$.

La recherche sur l'analyse diophantienne entière ne s'est pas arrêtée avec ses initiateurs de la première moitié du Xe siècle. Bien au contraire, leurs successeurs la reprennent ensuite, dans le même esprit d'abord. Au terme de cette évolution, on voit croître de plus en plus le recours aux moyens purement arithmétiques dans l'étude des équations diophantiennes [1].

À travers cet exemple de l'analyse diophantienne, j'ai voulu montrer par une illustration comment l'algèbre conçue avec al-Khwārizmī fut centrale pour la fondation et la transformation de cette nouvelle discipline. La dialectique entre algèbre et arithmétique a permis, nous l'avons vu, de fonder l'analyse diophantienne rationnelle comme partie de l'algèbre; ainsi désormais, d'al-Karajī à Euler, un traité d'algèbre important comprend un chapitre sur l'analyse diophantienne rationnelle. D'autre part, nous avons

---

(1) R. Rashed, "Al-Yazdī et l'équation $\sum_{i=1}^{n} x_i^2 = x^2$", *Historia Scientiarum*, vol. 4-2 (1994), p. 79-101.

assisté à la naissance de l'analyse diophantienne entière, destinée à répondre aux exigences de la démonstration. Nous avons enfin vu surgir avec ces disciplines les éléments d'une nouvelle rationalité mathématique, qui admet l'infinité des solutions comme solution véritable, qui permet de différencier entre plusieurs types d'infinité de solutions – les identités et le nombre infiniment grand – et de considérer positivement l'impossibilité, c'est-à-dire la solution impossible comme objet de construction et de démonstration[1]. Or tous ces traits sont précisément ceux de l'analyse diophantienne classique, telle qu'elle fut conçue et pratiquée au XVIIe siècle par Bachet de Méziriac et Fermat. Ce dernier invente vers 1640 la méthode de la descente infinie[2], qui à son tour renouvellera la discipline; ceci est une autre histoire.

Mais on peut s'interroger: à cette continuité épistémologique pour ainsi dire correspond-il une certaine continuité historique, et laquelle? Plus concrètement, Bachet de Méziriac est-il, au début du XVIIe siècle, une création *ex nihilo*? Arrêtons-nous quelque peu à cette question, qui intéresse notre propos ici. Ma réponse consistera simplement à rappeler une figure, celle du plus important des mathématiciens du Moyen Âge latin et la source de bien des écrits de la Renaissance: Fibonacci, *alias* Leonardo Pisano.

---

(1) R. Rashed, *Entre arithmétique et algèbre*, p. 195 sqq.

(2) J. Itard, *Essais d'histoire des mathématiques* (réunis et traduits par R. Rashed), Paris, 1984, pp. 229-234.

Fibonacci, qui a résidé à Bougie (1170-après 1240) et voyagé en Syrie, en Égypte et en Sicile, était en rapport avec l'Empereur Frédéric II et sa cour. Cette cour comprenait des arabisants, qui s'occupaient de mathématiques arabes, comme Jean de Palerme, ou simplement des arabophones qui s'y connaissaient en mathématiques, comme Théodore d'Antioche. Or Fibonacci a écrit en analyse diophantienne le *Liber Quadratorum*, que les historiens des mathématiques tiennent à juste titre comme la plus importante contribution du Moyen Âge latin en théorie des nombres, avant celles de Bachet de Méziriac et de Fermat. Le but de ce livre, de l'aveu même de Fibonacci, est de résoudre ce système

$$x^2 + 5 = y^2$$

$$x^2 - 5 = z^2$$

proposé par Jean de Palerme. Or il ne s'agit pas de n'importe quelle question d'analyse diophantienne, mais d'un problème qui apparaît en personne, à plusieurs reprises, dans les travaux d'al-Karajī et de bien d'autres. Plus généralement, les principaux résultats exposés dans le *Liber Quadratorum* sont ou bien ceux obtenus des mathématiciens arabes des X-XIe siècles, ou très proches de ceux-ci; et, bien plus, ils s'inscrivent dans un contexte mathématique identique: la théorie des triplets pythagoriciens. Cette conclusion

41

proposée ici n'est nullement nouvelle; un éminent historien dont l'admiration pour Fibonacci ne souffre aucun doute l'a déjà avancée: je veux parler de Gino Loria, qui écrit:

> S'il semble difficile de nier que Léonard de Pise a été conduit aux recherches qui viennent d'être résumées par l'exemple de Muḥammed ibn Ḥossein (lire al-Khāzin), sa dépendance à l'égard de celui-ci apparaît encore moins douteuse quand il s'agit de la section suivante du *Liber Quadratorum*, laquelle traite des "nombres congruents".

Le *Liber Quadratorum* appartient donc bien à cette tradition des mathématiciens du Xe siècle qui ont conçu l'analyse diophantienne entière.

Le cas de Fibonacci et de l'analyse diophantienne n'est pas unique, bien qu'exemplaire compte tenu du niveau atteint. Ce mathématicien qui, vu d'amont, serait une figure des mathématiques arabes des IXe-XIe siècles, est bien un savant des XVe-XVIIe siècles des mathématiques latines, vu d'aval.

Nous venons de voir sur cet exemple que la modernité scientifique classique prend ses racines au IXe siècle, et qu'elle s'est développée jusque tard dans le XVIIe siècle: c'est ainsi que l'analyse diophantienne rationnelle se prolonge jusqu'au XVIIIe siècle, alors que l'analyse diophantienne entière subit une nouvelle révolution au milieu du XVIIe siècle. Nous avons vu également que cette modernité est de langue arabe à ses débuts, qu'elle a été transmise par le latin, l'hébreu et l'italien, avant de s'engager dans de nouvelles recherches significatives; que son noyau rationnel, enfin, s'est formé dans l'algèbre, et que ses conditions de possibilité sont inhérentes à la nouvelle ontologie fournie par cette discipline.

Nous sommes, avec cette description, bien loin de l'attitude globale dominante, et le terme "Renaissance" paraît pour le moins inadéquat à rendre compte des faits.

Venons-en à présent au deuxième trait de la modernité scientifique classique, je veux parler des normes expérimentales comme normes de la preuve. Pour le dire en bref, l'atténuation du clivage entre science et art, et le changement des rapports entre les deux termes dans la civilisation islamique, autrement plus urbanisée que celles qui la précédaient, a eu pour principal effet l'extension de la recherche empirique, et la genèse d'une notion diffuse de l'expérimentation. Et de fait, l'usage systématique des procédés empiriques se multiplie alors: classifications des botanistes et des linguistes, par exemple; expériences de contrôle des médecins et expériences des alchimistes; observations cliniques et diagnostic comparé des médecins. Mais il fallait attendre que s'établissent de nouveaux rapports entre les mathématiques et la physique pour qu'une telle notion, encore diffuse, de l'expérimentation, se vît confier la dimension qui la détermine: une composante, à la fois systématique et réglée, de la preuve. Cette conception ne pouvait qu'être nouvelle, et ne devait pas se confondre avec celle de l'observation contrôlée, ni même mesurée, en astronomie. Il faut cette fois aménager le plan d'existence même des phénomènes examinés. Or c'est en optique qu'une telle conception a d'abord vu le jour, avant d'être élaborée en mécanique; elle émerge sous cette forme pour la première fois dans l'œuvre d'Ibn al-Haytham, notamment dans son livre *L'Optique*, traduit en latin au XIIᵉ siècle, et en italien plus tard. Réédité par Risner au XVIᵉ siècle, c'était le livre de référence pour tous les savants au Moyen Âge, aussi bien que pour Kepler, Descartes et Malebranche, parmi bien d'autres, par la suite [1].

Mais, pour comprendre l'émergence de cette nouvelle norme et de cette nouvelle pratique, rappelons très brièvement le projet d'Ibn al-Haytham. Celui-ci poursuit dans l'ensemble de ses écrits la réalisation d'un programme de réforme de la discipline, qui l'a précisément amené à reprendre tour à tour les différents domaines: optique, optique météorologique, catoptrique, miroirs ardents, dioptrique, sphère ardente, optique physique. L'acte fondateur de cette réforme consistait à faire clairement le départ entre les conditions de propagation de la lumière et les conditions de la vision des objets. Elle a conduit d'une part à doter d'un support physique les règles de la

---

(1) Sur les travaux optiques d'Ibn al-Haytham, voir notre *Optique et mathématiques : recherches sur la pensée scientifique en arabe*, Variorum, Aldershot, 1992; et *Géométrie et Dioptrique au Xᵉ siècle. Ibn Sahl, al-Qūhī et Ibn al-Haytham*, Paris, Les Belles-Lettres, 1993.

propagation - il s'agit d'une analogie mathématiquement assurée entre un modèle mécanique du mouvement d'une balle solide lancée contre un obstacle, et celui de la lumière - et d'autre part, à partout procéder géométriquement, et par expérimentation. L'optique n'a plus le sens qu'elle revêtait naguère chez les Grecs: une géométrie de la perception. Elle comprend désormais deux parties: une théorie de la vision, à laquelle sont également associées une physiologie de l'œil et une psychologie de la perception, et une théorie de la lumière, à laquelle sont liées une optique géométrique et une optique physique. Cette réforme a abouti, entre autres, à l'émergence de problèmes neufs, jamais posés auparavant, comme par exemple l'examen de la lentille sphérique et du dioptre sphérique, non seulement en tant qu'instruments ardents, mais en tant qu'instruments optiques, en dioptrique. Elle a aussi abouti à la création d'une nouvelle pratique d'investigation - et du nouveau lexique qui lui est associé - celle de l'expérimentation.

Mais, qu'entend Ibn al-Haytham par "expérimentation"? Nous trouverons chez Ibn al-Haytham autant de sens à ce mot, et autant de fonctions assurées par l'expérimentation, qu'il y a de rapports entre les mathématiques et la physique. Ceux-ci s'établissent en effet selon plusieurs modes qui, s'ils ne sont pas thématisés par Ibn al-Haytham, sont sous-jacents à son œuvre, et en permettent l'analyse.

Pour l'optique géométrique, dont la réforme est le fait d'Ibn al-Haytham, l'unique rapport entre mathématiques et physique est un isomorphisme de structures. Grâce à sa définition du rayon lumineux, en particulier, Ibn al-Haytham a pu concevoir les phénomènes de la propagation y compris le phénomène de la diffusion, de telle manière qu'ils épousent parfaitement la géométrie. Plusieurs montages expérimentaux sont alors inventés pour assurer le contrôle technique des propositions déjà contrôlées sur le plan linguistique par la géométrie. Ainsi par exemple les expériences destinées à éprouver les lois et les règles de l'optique géométrique. La lecture des travaux d'Ibn al-Haytham atteste en outre deux faits importants: tout d'abord, certaines expériences d'Ibn al-Haytham ne sont pas simplement destinées à contrôler des assertions qualitatives, mais aussi à obtenir des résultats quantitatifs; en second lieu, l'appareillage conçu par Ibn al-Haytham, varié, et pour l'époque, complexe, ne se réduit pas à celui des astronomes.

En optique physique, on rencontre un autre type de rapports entre mathématiques et physique, et, par suite, un deuxième sens du terme "expérimentation". L'intervention des mathématiques s'effectue à ce stade par l'entremise des analogies établies entre les schémas du mouvement d'un corps grave et ceux de la réflexion et de la réfraction. Autrement dit, les mathématiques sont introduites dans l'optique physique par l'intermédiaire des schémas dynamiques du mouvement des corps graves, eux-mêmes supposés déjà mathématisés. C'est précisément cette mathématisation préalable des notions d'une doctrine physique qui a permis qu'elles fussent transférées sur le plan d'une situation expérimentale. Provisoire, certes, cette situation n'en a pas moins fourni un plan d'existence à des notions syntactiquement structurées, mais sémantiquement indéterminées: tel le schéma des mouvements du projectile d'Ibn al-Haytham, repris par Kepler et Descartes.

Un troisième type d'expérimentation, non pratiquée par Ibn al-Haytham lui-même, mais rendu possible par sa propre réforme et par ses découvertes en optique, apparaît à la fin du XIIIe siècle chez son successeur al-Fārisī: les rapports instaurés entre mathématiques et physique visent, dans ce cas, à construire un modèle; par conséquent, à réduire systématiquement, au moyen de la géométrie, la propagation de la lumière dans un milieu naturel à sa propagation dans un objet fabriqué. Il s'agit donc de définir, pour la propagation, entre l'objet naturel et l'objet fabriqué, des correspondances analogiques véritablement assurées d'un statut mathématique: ainsi le modèle de la sphère massive en verre, remplie d'eau, pour l'explication de l'arc-en-ciel. L'expérimentation a donc ici pour fonction de réaliser les conditions physiques d'un phénomène que l'on ne peut étudier ni directement, ni complètement.

A ces trois types d'expérimentation, on pourrait en joindre d'autres. Retenons simplement que, en dépit de la différence des fonctions qu'elles assurent, les trois types d'expérimentation que nous venons d'étudier se présentent tous, à la différence de l'observation, et même de l'observation astronomique traditionnelle, non seulement comme moyen de contrôle, mais comme fournissant un plan d'existence à ces notions syntactiquement structurées. Il s'agit dans ces trois cas de situations où le savant entend réaliser lui-même physiquement son objet, pour pouvoir le penser; c'est, en un mot, un moyen de réaliser physiquement un objet de pensée non réalisable auparavant.

Or, la réforme d'Ibn al-Haytham aussi bien que les normes expérimentales requises comme partie intégrante de la preuve en physique, ont survécu à l'auteur. D'Ibn al-Haytham à Kepler, puis aux autres savants du XVIIe siècle, l'axe généalogique est ainsi établi. Sur ce terrain également, la connaissance de la science arabe est nécessaire à la compréhension de la modernité classique; elle permet de saisir l'introduction des normes expérimentales, mais aussi de mieux situer l'apparition tard dans le XVIIe siècle d'une autre dimension encore voilée de l'expérimentation: la recherche de la *précision*.

Pour conclure, rappelons donc les deux points centraux de cet exposé. Nous avons vu d'abord que les nouvelles possibilités offertes par l'algèbre étaient à l'origine d'une nouvelle stratégie et d'une nouvelle rationalité. Cette stratégie est inhérente au développement de l'algèbre elle-même après al-Khwārizmī, et dans ses rapports avec les autres disciplines mathématiques. Stratégie qui consiste, en algèbre, à exhiber de plus en plus les structures et les opérations, et, dans ses rapports avec les autres disciplines, à engager cette dialectique d'application que nous avons évoquée. Quant à la nouvelle rationalité, elle s'appuie sur une nouvelle ontologie de l'objet mathématique qui rend possible ce qui ne l'était pas auparavant: un seul et même objet est susceptible d'une détermination géométrique et d'une détermination arithmétique à la fois; un problème peut avoir une infinité de solutions vraies; une solution approchée est une solution vraie; une solution impossible est aussi une solution vraie; une même opération peut s'appliquer à des objets différents sans aucune justification supplémentaire, etc.

Nous avons également assisté à l'émergence de la nouvelle conception de la preuve en physique, et nous avons vu comment on admet désormais que le plan d'existence d'un objet physique n'est plus son plan "naturel", mais simplement celui de son montage expérimental.

Cette nouvelle rationalité, qui peut se dire en bref algébrique et expérimentale, et qui caractérise la modernité classique, a été fondée, nous l'avons dit, entre le IXe et le XIIe siècles, par les savants dispersés entre l'Espagne musulmane et les confins de la Chine, mais qui tous écrivaient en arabe. L'appropriation de cette nouvelle rationalité par les savants a commencé au

XIIᵉ siècle, et une nouvelle émulation verra le jour à partir du XVIᵉ siècle, donnant lieu à des perfectionnements. Il paraît donc indispensable, pour qui veut comprendre la modernité classique, de rompre avec cette périodisation tracée par les historiens, fondée sur un lien causal entre les événements de l'histoire politique, religieuse et littéraire de la Renaissance, et ceux de la science. Il faut donc retrouver les véritables trajectoires, et abandonner les légendes qui ont pu induire en erreur des esprits aussi grands que celui de Husserl.

العلم في الإسلام والحداثة الكلاسيكية

الأستاذ الدكتور رشدي راشد

منشورات الفرقان: رقم ٧١
سلسلة محاضرات مؤسسة الفرقان: رقم ٤

مؤسسة الفرقان للتراث الإسلامي

Al-Furqān Islamic Heritage Foundation
Eagle House
High Street
Wimbledon
London SW19 5EF U.K.
Tel: + 44 208 944 1233
Fax: + 44 208 944 1633
E-mail: info@al-furqan.com
http://www.al-furqan.com

ISBN 1 873992 71 8

منشورات الفرقان: رقم ٧١
سلسلة محاضرات مؤسسة الفرقان: رقم ٤

العلم في الإسلام والحداثة الكلاسيكية

الأستاذ الدكتور رشدي راشد

مؤسسة الفرقان للتراث الإسلامي

لنـــدن

١٤٢٣ / ٢٠٠٢

نبذة عن الأستاذ الدكتور رشدي راشد

رشدي راشد مدير أبحاث بالمركز الوطني الفرنسي للبحث العلمي وأستاذ متقاعد من جامعة طوكيو وهو مدير لعدة مراكز للأبحاث في تاريخ العلوم وفلسفاتها. نشر أبحاثاً عديدة في تاريخ الرياضيات وفلسفتها، وتاريخ المناظر، وتاريخ تطبيق الرياضيات على العلوم الاجتماعية، وفي تاريخ الرياضيات والعلوم في الحضارة الإسلامية.

أصدرت له مؤسسة الفرقان للتراث الإسلامي **تاريخ الرياضيات التحليلية بين القرن الثالث والخامس للهجرة**، وهو حائز على العديد من الميداليات والأوسمة، وعضو في عدد من الأكاديميات العلمية، وهو عضو مجلس الخبراء بمؤسسة الفرقان.

العلم في الإسلام والحداثة الكلاسيكية

رشدي راشد

متى كانت النهضة؟

كتب الفيلسوف الألماني هوسيرل (E. Husserl) في عام ١٩٣٦ بأسلوبه المعتاد « من المعروف أنه خلال فترة النهضة انقلبت البشرية الأوروبية انقلابا ثوريا على أساليب الحياة التى كانت سائدة في العصور الوسطى، والتي لم تعد تعتز بها، بل فضلت عليها نوعا جديدا من الحرية»[1]. إن تعبير "النهضة" لدى هوسيرل لا يشير إلى ذلك المفهوم كما كان يستخدم في الدوائر الأدبية وتلك ذات النزعة الإنسانية (humanist) الإيطالية في القرن الخامس عشر، ولا إلى المفهوم كما يرد لاحقا في كتابات أرازمس (حيث يتعلق أساسا بتجديد التعليم والدين)، وإنما يشير إلى مفهوم متعلق بالعلم وبالفلسفة التي لا تنفصل عنه، وهو مفهوم ازداد تبلورا في نهاية القرن السادس عشر

---

(1) Husserl, *La crise des sciences européennes et la phénoménologie transcendantale*, tr. G. Garnel, Paris, 1976, p. 12.

وخلال القرن السابع عشر؛ لذلك يبدو مفهوم النهضة ـ في هذا السياق ـ مرتبطا بالعلم الكلاسيكي (باكورة العلم الحديث)، ويصبو المفهوم إلى أن يكون في آن سلاحا وأداة تفسير أو على الأقل أداة وصف. استخدم علماء القرن السابع عشر وفلاسفته مفهوم النهضة كسلاح للتأكيد على الاختلاف ـ الحقيقي أو الوهمي ـ بينهم وبين الأقدمين ولتعزيز مساهمتهم الخاصة، يظهر ذلك جليا إذا ما فكرنا في بيكون أو ديكارت أو جاليليو، أما كأداة وصف أو تفسير فمصطلح "النهضة" ـ كما يؤكد هوسيرل ـ ليس مجرد وسيلة تقليدية للإشارة إلى حقبة زمنية، وإنما هو وصف لتلك اللحظة الفريدة التي قامت فيها حركة التحرر الفكري الأوروبية بانتزاع نفسها من الجهل والخرافة.

إن ادعاءات هوسيرل لا تتناقض مع ما كان سائدا في عصره، فغيره من الفلاسفة والمؤرخين يؤمنون أيضا بأن "النهضة" و"الإصلاح" و"الثورة العلمية" هي أنسب المفاهيم لوصف الحداثة الكلاسيكية، ويوجد شبه إجماع على هذا التصور الذي ترجع جذوره إلى القرن الثامن عشر، إذ بدأ استخدامه منذ ذلك الوقت لتقديم مفهوم "التقدم اللانهائي" كما في أفكار ويليم وتون (William Wotton) في إنجلترا وفونتنيل (Fontenelle) في فرنسا. وفي القرن التاسع عشر أضافت الحركة

الرومانسية الألمانية لهذا التصور بعدا أنثروبولوجيا . بغض النظر عن جذور هذا التصور فهو يطرح سؤالا محوريا حول أصل وتطور الحداثة الكلاسيكية يرتبط ارتباطا وثيقا بالعلم وفلسفته.

خلف ستار الإجماع الظاهري بدأ التصور الذي تحدثنا عنه يتعرض للهجوم على يد بيير دوهم (Pierre Duhem) رغم أنه أحد مفكري المدرسة الفيلولوجية الألمانية. كان بيير دوهم عالم فيزياء فرنسيا مرموقا، كما كان مؤرخا للعلم اللاتيني في العصور الوسطى، وجعلته فلسفته للعلوم وكذلك قناعاته الدينية والسياسية أكثر إدراكا من غيره للاستمرارية التاريخية، كما جعلته أكثر انجذابا نحو العصور الوسطى، لذا نجده يؤرخ للحداثة الكلاسيكية بداية من اللاتينيين في القرن الرابع عشر، أي كلية ميرتون بأكسفورد وجامعة باريس. وقد نقد هذه الأطروحة عدد من مؤرخي الأفكار العلمية مثل هاسكينز (.C.H Haskins) وكويريه (A.Koyré) وسـارتون (G. Sarton)... الخ، كما انتقدتها بطريقة مغايرة أناليز ماير (Anneliese Maier) في أعمالها المتميزة، ومؤخرا حاول مارشال كلاجيت (Marshall Clagett) أن يعيد التوازن بين الفرقاء، لكن أظهرت هذه المناظرة ـ وجهود العديد من الباحثين خلال القرن العشرين ـ أن مفاهيم مثل "النهضة"

و"الإصلاح" و"الثورة العلمية" تعجز عن تفسير الوقائع المتراكمة، وأن دور القرن الرابع عشر في تطور العلم الكلاسيكي يبهت إذا ما قورن بالقرنين الثاني عشر والثالث عشر حين بدأ اللاتينيون استيعاب العلم الهيليني والعربي، وقد وقع هذا قبل "النهضة" بثلاثة قرون. ومن ثم يثبت أن الأساليب التقليدية في تقسيم العصور السياسية أو الثقافية لا تفيد كثيرا في محاولة فهم وتحليل الحداثة الكلاسيكية، وتغيب عن تلك المناظرة الأعمال الإسلامية الأصيلة وإن كانت حاضرة دائما من خلال ترجماتها اللاتينية.

العلم في الإسلام

أنتقل الآن إلى موضوع العلم في الإسلام (دون أن نقتصر على ترجماته اللاتينية) والعلم الكلاسيكي، حيث أهدف إلى بيان أن مزيدا من المعرفة بالعلم العربي تسهم في تحسين قدرتنا على فهم العلم الكلاسيكي من الناحيتين الإبستيمولوجية والتاريخية. سننظر في خاصتين مميزتين للعلم الكلاسيكي:

(ا) عقلانية رياضية جديدة،

(ب) التجريب كنمط من أنماط البرهان.

العقلانية الرياضية الجديدة

وللنظر الآن ليس إلى أحد الفلاسفة مثل هوسيرل وإنما إلى حلاق بسيط، هو حلاق بغداد الذي يقول في **ألف ليلة وليلة**: [1]

« ... ستجدني أحسن حلاق في بغداد، حكيم مجرب وصيدلي عميق ومنجم لا يخطئ، ضليع في النحو والبلاغة ومؤهل في علوم الرياضة في الهندسة والحساب وكل مسائل الجبر، في التاريخ أعرف تاريخ الممالك في العالم، بالإضافة إلى ذلك أعرف جميع أبواب الفلسفة وأحفظ في ذاكرتي كل القوانين والتقاليد، وأنا أيضا شاعر ومهندس ...»

يتضح من هذا أن كل من الرياضيات والجبر كان يشغل مكانا مميزا في الموسوعة الدارجة للمعارف في المدن الكبيرة في ذلك العصر، ويذكر الجبر ككيان قائم بذاته؛ فكلمات الحلاق هي أصداء لتصنيفات العلوم كما ترد لدى من هم أكثر علما ومنهم على سبيل المثال لا الحصر الفارابي فيلسوف القرن العاشر أو ابن سينا في القرن الذي يليه، فقد اختلفت تلك التصنيفات عن نظيرتها اليونانية إذ احتفت بذلك العلم الجديد وأطلقت عليه اسما يخصه هو: الجبر. فالاهتمام العام بالرياضيات وانتشارها الواسع والمكانة المميزة للجبر فيها هي سمات لما يمكن أن نسميه العلم العربي.

---

(1) *Les Mille et une Nuits*, tr. A. Galland, ed. Garnier-Flammarion, [I, p. 426-7].

لنعد إلى بغداد في بدايات القرن التاسع كي نلقي نظرة سريعة على أصل تكوين السمات الأساسية لتلك الرياضيات العربية. في تلك الفترة وصلت عملية ترجمة أعمال الرياضيات الهيلينية العظيمة أوجها، وتميزت بسمتين لافتتين:

(١) قام بالترجمة علماء رياضيات، ـ كثيرا ما كانوا من أبرز العلماء ـ وكان الدافع للترجمة هو أكثر الأبحاث تقدما في ذلك العصر.

(٢) لم تكن دوافع البحث نظرية فقط، بل شملت أيضا احتياجات المجتمع الجديد في مجالات مثل علوم الفلك والبصريات والحساب وكذلك آلات القياس المستحدثة...الخ. كانت بدايات القرن التاسع فترة توسع هامة في الرياضيات الهيلينية بالعربية، وفي تلك الفترة بالذات ومن داخل نخبة العلماء في "بيت الحكمة" في بغداد كتب محمد ابن موسى الخوارزمي كتابا في موضوع جديد، بأسلوب جديد، وفي صفحات هذا الكتاب ظهر الجبر لأول مرة كفرع مميز ومستقل من فروع الرياضيات، كان الحدث حاسما، وقد أدرك معاصرو الخوارزمي ذلك، ويرجع ذلك إلى طبيعة الموجودات التي استحدثت كموضوع للدراسة بقدر ما يرجع الأسلوب الرياضي المتبع، فأسلوب العرض يعطي متتابعة الخطوات التي يجب اتباعها للوصول إلى الحل (خواريزم الحل كما يسمى الآن)، كما يعطي البرهان على صحة الحل الذي

نحصل عليه عن طريق تلك الخطوات. وتظهر منذ ذلك الوقت مؤشرات على تلك الإمكانية الهائلة الكامنة في الرياضيات التي ستسود الرياضيات من القرن التاسع فصاعدا، ألا وهي تطبيق فروع الرياضيات المختلفة على بعضها البعض، فقد أتاح أسلوب الجبر وعموم مقاصده هذه التطبيقات التي ستعدل ـ بكثرتها وتنوعها ـ بنية الرياضيات باستمرار بعد القرن التاسع. هكذا ولدت عقلانية رياضية جديدة، ونعتقد أن هذه العقلانية تميز الرياضيات الكلاسيكية والعلم الكلاسيكي عموما.

بدأ خلفاء الخوارزمي رويدا يطبقون الحساب على الجبر، والجبر على الحساب، وكليهما على حساب المثلثات، وكذلك طبقوا الجبر على نظرية الأعداد لإقليدس وعلى الهندسة كما طبقوا الهندسة على الجبر. وضعت بهذه التطبيقات أسس فروع أو على الأقل مباحث جديدة، فصار لدينا جبر كثيرات الحدود والتحليل التوافيقي والتحليل العددي والحلول العددية التقريبية للمعادلات، ونظرية الأعداد الجديدة والبناء الهندسي للمعادلات، وهذه التطبيقات المتعددة لها أيضا نتائج أخرى مثل فصل موضوع التحليل الديوفانتيني في نطاق الأعداد الصحيحة عن التحليل الديوفانتيني في نطاق الأعداد القياسية، وهذا الأخير سيصير لاحقا مبحثا مستقلا من مباحث الجبر.

وهكذا نرى كيف تغيرت الرياضيات بدءا من القرن التاسع واتسع أفقها، فنرى أولا التوسعات في الهندسة الهيلينية والحساب الهيليني

مثل: نظرية القطاعات المخروطية، ونظرية المتوازيات والدراسات الإسقاطية والطرق الأرشيميدية لقياس السطوح والحجوم المنحنية، ومسائل الأشكال ذات المحيطات المتساوية والتحويلات الهندسية؛ فتصبح جميع هذه المجالات موضوعا لدراسات يقوم بها علماء مرموقون منهم على سبيل المثال لا الحصر ثابت بن قرة وابن سهل وابن الهيثم، وينجح هؤلاء العلماء بعد دراسات متعمقة في تطوير تلك المواضيع على نهج من سبقوهم أو في تحويرها وتعديلها متى اقتضت الضرورة ذلك. ومن داخل تراث الرياضيات الهيلينية هذا نرى بداية استكشاف مواضيع رياضية ليست هيلينية.

هكذا ستتغير رويدا مكونات الرياضيات ـ لغتها وتقنياتها ومعاييرها ـ حتى تظهر في صورة جديدة نتأملها من خلال مثالين: التحليل الديوفانتيني في نطاق الأعداد المنطقة والتحليل الديوفانتيني في نطاق الأعداد الصحيحة.

التحليل الديوفانتيني المنطق

يرجع بزوغ التحليل الديوفانتيني كمبحث مستقل إلى خلفاء الخوارزمي وبالذات إلى أبي كامل الذي كتب كتابه حوالي عام ٨٨٠ وقد ترجم

الكتاب إلى اللاتينية في القرن الثاني عشر وإلى العبرية في القرن الخامس عشر في إيطاليا.

يهدف أبو كامل في كتاب **الجبر** إلى تطوير ما ورد في الأعمال السابقة، وإلى إعطاء عرض منظم لا يكتفي بالمسائل وخوارزميات حلها، وإنما يكشف عن المنهج كذلك، فقرب نهاية **الجبر** يعالج أبو كامل ٣٨ مسألة ديوفانتينية من الدرجة الثانية، وأنظمة تلك المعادلات، وأربعة أنظمة لمعادلات خطية ليس لها حل وحيد، وأنظمة أخرى من المعدلات الخطية ذات الحل الوحيد، ومجموعة من المسائل التي تدور حول المتواليات الحسابية، ومزيد من الدراسة لهذا النوع من المعادلات.[1] تحقق تلك المجموعة من المسائل الهدف المزدوج لأبي كامل: حل المسائل التي لها عدد لا نهائي من الحلول، واستخدام الجبر في حل مسائل جرت العادة على أن يعالجها علماء الحساب. يظهر في **الجبر** لأبي كامل ـ في حدود علمي ـ لأول مرة في التاريخ التمييز الصريح بين المسائل التي لها عدد منتهي من الحلول، وتلك التي لها عدد لا نهائي من الحلول. إن دراسة مسائل أبي كامل الديوفانتينية للثمانية والثلاثين مسألة تكشف هذا التمييز وتكشف أيضا أن تتابع

---

(1) Istanbul, MS Kara Mustafa Paşa n 379, fol. 79r-110v.

المسائل ليس عشوائيا، بل إنها تتبع ترتيب يشير إليه أبو كامل ضمنا، فيضع المسائل الخمس والعشرين الأولى في مجموعة واحدة ويعطي شرطا لازما وكافيا لتحديد الحلول المنطقة الموجبة، مثلا:

$$x^2 + 5 = y^2$$

يحول أبو كامل المسألة إلى مسألة تقسيم عدد ـ هو مجموع مربعين ـ إلى مربعين آخرين، ويحل تلك الأخيرة. وتدل تقنية الحل على إدراك أبي كامل أنه إذا أمكن التعبير عن أحد المتغيرين كدالة منطقة في الآخر أو بشكل أعم إذا أمكن أيجاد تعبير (بارمتري) قياسي عن المتغيرين فكل الحلول ممكنة، بينما إذا أدى المجموع إلى تعبير ذي جذر أصم فلا توجد حلول على الإطلاق. بتعبير آخر لا يعرفه أبو كامل فإن المنحني من الدرجة الثانية إما أن يكون بلا أي نقطة منطقة أو أن يكون مكافئً منطقيًا bi-rationally للخط المستقيم.

تتكون المجموعة الثانية من ثلاثة عشر مسألة يستحيل التعبير (البارمتري) القياسي عنها، ومرة أخرى باستخدام لغة لا يعرفها أبو كامل، تعين تلك المسائل جميعا منحنيات من الجنس ١ 1(genus) كما في:

$$x^2 + \text{x} = y^2$$
$$x^2 + 1 = z^2$$

التي تعين منحنى منحرف من الدرجة الرابعة (skew quartic) في A^3

من الجنس ١.

وبعد نصف قرن سيتوسع عالم جبر آخر هو الكرجي في التحليل الديوفانتيني القياسي بشكل غير مسبوق. وضع الكرجي علامة هامة في تاريخ الجبر إذ عرف كثيرات الحدود والحساب الجبري على كثيرات الحدود، ويختلف الكرجي عن سابقيه ـ من ديوفانتيس إلى أبي كامل ـ في التحليل الديوفانتيني القياسي، فلم يعط قوائم بالمسائل وحلولها مثل قوائمهم، بل نظم عرضه على أساس عدد الحدود في العبارة الجبرية والفروق بين قوى تلك الحدود، فمثلا يعالج الكرجي على التوالي:

$$ax^{2n} \pm bx^{2n-1} = y^2$$

ثم $ax^{2n} + bx^{2n-2} = y^2$

ثم $ax^2 + bx + c = y^2$

وحذا خلفاؤه حذوه في أسلوب التنظيم هذا. من ناحية أخرى تقدم الكرجي في أداء المهمة التي بدأها أبو كامل، حيث يحاول بقدر الإمكان كشف المنهج المستخدم لحل كل نمط من المسائل. ونشير إلى

المسألة:

$$x^2 + a = y^2$$

$$x^2 - b = z^2$$

التي تعين منحنى في A^3 من الجنس ١.

وقد حاول خلفاء الكرجي أن يسيروا على نهجه، لكننا سنكتفي بهذا القدر فيما يخص التحليل الديوفانتيني القياسي بالعربية لنلقي نظرة على تطور التحليل الديوفانتيني في مجال الأعداد الصحيحة.

التحليل الديوفانتيني في مجال الأعداد الصحيحة

يمكن القول أن التحليل الديوفانتيني في مجال الأعداد الصحيحة ـ أو التحليل الديوفانتيني الجديد ـ تأسس للمرة الأولى خلال القرن العاشر بفضل الجبر ورغما عنه في نفس الوقت، فمن جانب بدأت محاولة البحث عن حلول للمسائل الديوفانتينية من بين الأعداد الصحيحة، ومن جانب آخر استخدم نهج الفصول الحسابية من كتاب **الأصول** لإقليدس، وقد سمح هذا المزج ـ الذي حدث لأول مرة في التاريخ ـ بين عالم الأعداد الصحيحة الموجبة (منظورا إليها كقطع خطوط مستقيمة) والتقنيات الجبرية والبراهين ذات الطابع الإقليدي الصرف تحديدا بولادة التحليل الديوفانتيني الجديد. نعلم أن ترجمة كتاب

ديوفانتيس **المسائل العددية** لم توفر لهؤلاء الرياضيين مناهج للحل،
بقدر ما أعطتهم مجموعة من المسائل في نظرية الأعداد صيغت في
ذلك الكتاب، وعلى خلاف سابقهم السكندري شرعوا على الفور في
تبويب هذه المسائل وفحصها: تمثيل العدد المكون من مجموع
مربعات، والأعداد المنسجمة ... (congruent numbers) الخ.

لنرى كيف درس رياضي من القرن العاشر مثل الخازن المثلثات القائمة
العددية ومسائل الأعداد المنسجمة، يعطي الخازن حل مسألة الأعداد
المنسجمة بطريق مكافئة لما يلي [1]:

ليكن لدينا عدد طبيعي a، الشروط التالية متكافئة:

1- نظام المعادلات $x^2 + a = y^2,$

$x^2 - a = z^2$

له حل

2- يوجد زوج من الأعداد الصحيحة (m, n) بحيث

$m^2 + n^2 = x^2$

$2mn = a$

تحت هذه الشروط يكون a على صورة. $4uv\ (u^2 - v^2)$

(1)   R. Rashed, *Entre arithmétique et algèbre: Recherches sur l'histoire des mathématiques arabes*, Paris, 1984, p. 212, English transl. *The Development of Arabic Mathematics: Between Arithmetic and Algebra*, Kluwer, Boston Studies in Philosophy of Science, 1994.

في هذا السياق بدأت أيضا دراسة تمثيل العدد الصحيح كمجموع مربعات، ويخصص الخازن عدة نظريات في أطروحته لهذا الموضوع، كما كان رياضيو القرن العاشر هؤلاء أول من عالج المسائل المستحيلة مثل الحالة الأولى من نظرية فيرما (Fermat)، وبالرغم من هذا لم يتوقف الرياضيون عن الاهتمام بتلك المسألة، بل أعلنوا لاحقا استحالة الحالة الثانية. $x^4 + y^4 = z^4$

لم يتوقف البحث في التحليل الديوفانتيني في مجال الأعداد الصحيحة بوفاة مؤسسيه بعد منتصف القرن العاشر، بل على العكس استمر من خلفوهم في تطويره بنفس الروح في البداية، ولكن في نهاية تطوره بدأ يسود استخدام الأساليب الحسابية لمعالجة المعادلات الديوفانتينية.[1]

التقليد يستمر

قصدت بهذا العرض لمثال التحليل الديوفانتيني أن أوضح كيف لعب الجبر ـ الذي ولد في زمن الخوارزمي ـ دورا محوريا في تأسيس هذا الفرع الجديد وفي التحولات التي طرأت عليه، وكما رأينا فقد أمكن

---

(1) R. Rashed, "Al-Yazdī et l'équation $\sum_{i=1}^{n} x_i^2 = x^2$", *Historia Scientiarum*, vol. 4-2 (1994), pp. 79-101.

تأسيس التحليل الديوفانتيني المنطق كجزء من الجبر من خلال جدلية الجبر والحساب، ومنذ ذلك الوقت، من الخازن حتى أويلر (Euler) سيحتوي كل كتاب هام في الجبر على فصل في التحليل الديوفانتيني المنطق. في هذه المرحلة يولد التحليل الديوفانتيني في مجال الأعداد الصحيحة، ويكون على هذا المبحث الامتثال لمتطلبات البرهان، وتظهر مع هذه المباحث عقلانية رياضية جديدة؛ تعترف بالحلول التي عددها لا نهائي كحل أصيل للمسألة، ويتيح لنا هذا الوضع أن نفرق بين أنواع متعددة من حالات الحلول التي عددها لانهائي ـ مثال ذلك التفرقة بين المتطابقات وبين غيرها من الحالات التي يكون فيها عدد الحلول لا نهائيا ـ كما يتيح لنا أن ندرس بشكل إيجابي الحالات التي يستحيل فيها الحل كموضوع للبناء والبرهان.[1] وسنجد أن كل هذه السمات هي ما ميز التحليل الديوفانتيني كما تصوره كل من باشيه دو ميزيراك (Bachet de Meziriac) في القرن السابع عشر وفيرما، حتى أعطى فيرما في حوالي ١٦٤٠ روحا جديدة لهذا المبحث حين اخترع أسلوب التناقص اللانهائي (method of infinite descent)[2]، ولكن هذه قصة أخرى.

(1) R. Rashed, *Entre arithmétique et algèbre*, p. 195 sqq.

(2) J. Itard, *Essais d'histoire des mathématiques* (قدمها رشدي راشد) Paris, 1984, pp. 229-234.

ما وصفنا أعلاه يمكن تسميته بالاستمرارية المعرفية، والسؤال الذي
يطرح نفسه الآن هو هل تناظر تلك الاستمرارية المعرفية استمرارية
تاريخية؟ وما هي تلك الاستمرارية؟ لكي أجيب على هذا السؤال أذكر
بفيبوناتشي (Fibonacci) المعروف أيضا بليوناردو بيزانو (Pisano
Leonardo)، وهو من أهم رياضيي العصور الوسطى اللاتينيين
ومصدر العديد من كتابات النهضة.

عاش فيبوناتشي (من ١١٧٠ إلى ما بعد ١٢٤٠)، في الجزائر وسافر إلى
سورية ومصر وصقلية، وكان على اتصال بالإمبراطور فريدريك الثاني
وبلاطه، وكان في هذا البلاط عدد من دارسي العربية المهتمين
بالرياضيات العربية مثل جون أوف باليرمو (John of Palermo)
ومتحدثي العربية الملمين بالرياضيات مثل ثيودور الأنطاكي
(Theodore of Antioch). كتب فيبوناتشي في التحليل الديوفانتيني
كتاب Liber Quadratorum الذي يراه مؤرخو الرياضيات عن حق أهم
إسهام في نظرية الأعداد في العصور الوسطى اللاتينية قبل إسهامات
Bachet de Meziriac وفيرما. والغرض الذي يعلنه فيبوناتشي نفسه
لكتابه هو حل نظام المعادلات:

$$x^2 + 5 = y^2$$

$$x^2 - 5 = z^2$$

الذي عرضه عليه جون أوف باليرمو. وهذه المسألة بالذات من مسائل التحليل الديوفانتيني تكرر ظهورها مرارا في أعمال الكرجي وكثيرين غيره، وعموما فإن أهم النتائج التي تظهر في *Liber Quadratorum* هي ذات النتائج التي حصل عليها الرياضيون العرب في القرنين العاشر والحادي عشر أو تشبهها إلى حد كبير، بالإضافة إلى ذلك وضعت تلك النتائج في ذات السياق الرياضي وهو نظرية الثلاثيات الفيثاغورثية (Pythagorean triplets)، ونستنتج من هذا ما سبق أن كتبه جينو لوريا (Gino Loria) ـ وهو مؤرخ بارز لا يمكن التشكيك في إعجابه بفيبوناتشي ـ:

يصعب إنكار أن ليوناردو أوف بيزا (بيزانو) اقتيد إلى بحث سبق أن لخصه (محمد بن حسين الخازن)، ويظهر اعتماده عليه بجلاء في الجزء اللاحق من *Liber Quadratorum* حيث يعالج الأعداد المتجانسة.

مما سبق نرى أن كتاب *Liber Quadratorum* ينتمي بحق إلى المدرسة العلمية لرياضيي القرن العاشر الذين أبدعوا التحليل الديوفانتيني في نطاق الأعداد الصحيحة.

ليست حالة فيبوناتشي حالة فريدة، ولكن يمكننا القول أنها حالة نموذجية إذا أخذنا في الاعتبار المستوى الذي وصلت إليه، فمن منظور معين يبدو هذا الرياضي أحد عظماء الرياضيات العربية بين القرنين التاسع والحادي عشر، بينما يبدو من منظور آخر كأحد علماء الرياضيات اللاتينية بين القرن الخامس عشر والسابع عشر.

أوضح لنا المثال السابق كيف عادت جذور الحداثة العلمية الكلاسيكية إلى القرن التاسع وكيف استمرت تتطور حتى نهايات القرن السابع عشر، ويستمر التحليل الديوفانتيني المنطق على نفس المنوال في القرن الثامن عشر، بينما يتغير التحليل الديوفانتيني في نطاق الأعداد الصحيحة تغيرا جذريا في منتصف القرن السابع عشر. ورأينا أيضا كيف كانت لغة تلك الحداثة في بداياتها هي العربية، وكيف انتقلت من خلال اللاتينية والعبرية والإيطالية، قبل أن تصبح جزءا من أبحاث جديدة ذات شأن، وأخيرا رأينا كيف كان الجبر هو النواة العقلية لتلك الحداثة وأن شروط وجودها كانت متأصلة في الموجودات الجديدة التي حواها هذا الفرع.

يبتعد بنا السرد السابق عن المواقف السائدة، ويظهر مصطلح "النهضة" عاجزا عن وصف حقائق الرياضيات.

التجريب كنمط من أنماط البرهان

لنتأمل الآن السمة الثانية من سمات الحداثة العلمية الكلاسيكية؛ ألا وهي المعايير التجريبية كمعايير للبرهان، باختصار نتج عن تضييق الفجوة بين العلم والفن وتغير العلاقة بينهما في الحضارة الإسلامية ـ وهي حضارة كان دور المدينة فيها أكبر بكثير من الحضارات السابقة عليها ـ توسع في البحث التجريبي كما تولد تصور مبهم للتجريب، ومنذ ذلك الوقت تزايد الاستخدام المنتظم للإجراءات التجريبية؛ مثال ذلك التصنيفات في علمي النبات واللغة، وتجارب السيمياء، والتجارب الضابطة والمشاهدات الإكلينيكية والتشخيص المقارن عند الأطباء، ومع ذلك كان من الضروري تأسيس علاقات جديدة بين الرياضيات والفيزياء حتى يأخذ مفهوم التجريب ـ الذي لم يزل مبهما ـ وضعه كمكون منهجي من مكونات البرهان. كان ذلك مفهوما جديدا تماما، ولا يجوز الخلط بينه وبين المشاهدات المنضبطة أو حتى ذات القياسات في الفلك، إذ صار ضروريا أن تؤخذ في الاعتبار الطبيعة الوجودية ذاتها للظواهر محل الفحص. كان علم البصريات أول مبحث يظهر فيه مثل هذا التصور ثم تبلور أكثر في الميكانيكا، وقد ظهر أول ما ظهر في كتابات ابن الهيثم وبالذات في كتاب **المناظر** الذي ترجم إلى اللاتينية

في القرن الثاني عشر ثم إلى الإيطالية، وأعاد ريزنر (Risner) إصدارة في القرن السادس عشر، وكان مرجعا لكل باحثي العصور الوسطى، ثم كبلر (Kepler) وديكارت (Descartes) والبرانش (Malebranche) في زمن لاحق.[1]

كي نتفهم ظهور المعايير والممارسات الجديدة يجب أن نعود في عجالة إلى مشروع ابن الهيثم. كان ابن الهيثم مشغولا بإصلاح منظومة علم البصريات وهو ما دفعه إلى مراجعة مجالاته المختلفة واحدا بعد الآخر: المناظر والظواهر الضوئية الطبيعية وانعكاس الأشعة الضوئية والمرايا المحرقة وانكسار الأشعة الضوئية والكرة المحرقة، وعلم البصريات الفيزيائي. المسألة الجوهرية في هذا الإصلاح كانت التمييز بين القوانين التي تحكم انتشار الضوء والقوانين التي تحكم إبصار الأشياء، أدى هذا الإصلاح من ناحية إلى إعطاء سند فيزيائي لقوانين انتشار الضوء ـ هو ذلك التماثل الرياضي الفعلي بين النموذج الميكانيكي لحركة كرة تتصادم مع حاجز وبين الحركة الشبيهة لأشعة الضوء ـ ومن ناحية أخرى أدى إلى استخدام الأساليب الهندسية

---

[1] حول كتابات ابن الهيثم فى البصريات انظر مؤلفاتنا:

Optique et Mathématiques: recherches sur la pensée scientifique en arabe, Variorum, Aldershot, 1992.
Géométrie et Dioptrique au Xe siècle. Ibn Sahl, al-Qūhī et Ibn al-Haytham, Paris, Les Belles-Lettres, 1993.

والتجريب في كل مكان. تغير معنى علم البصريات ولم يعد يعني ما كان يعنيه لليونانيين ـ أي هندسة المنظور ـ بل صار مكونا من جزأين: أولا نظرية للإبصار، يرتبط بها أيضا تركيب العين وسيكولوجية الإدراك، وثانيا نظرية للضوء يرتبط بها علم المناظر الهندسي وعلم البصريات الفيزيائي، كما نتج عن هذا الإصلاح بروز أسئلة جديدة لم تكن قد صيغت من قبل ، مثال ذلك فحص العدسات الكروية والكاسر الكروي ـ من خلال دراسة الانكسار ـ بصفتها أدوات بصرية لا آلات حارقة. كما أدى هذا الإصلاح إلى ممارسة الدراسة بطريقة جديدة هي التجريب وظهور معجم جديد .

ماذا يعني "التجريب"(experimentation) عند ابن الهيثم؟ تتعدد معاني التجريب ووظائفه في أعمال ابن الهيثم بقدر تعدد العلاقات بين الرياضيات والفيزياء. يؤسس ابن الهيثم تلك العلاقات بمناهج متباينة وهو لا يعالج تلك المناهج كموضوع قائم بذاته إلا أنها موجودة بشكل ضمني في أعماله المختلفة يمكننا من تحليلها .

المساهمة الأساسية لابن الهيثم في مجال البصريات هي إصلاح علم المناظر الهندسي، والعلاقة الفريدة بين الرياضيات والفيزياء في علم المناظر الهندسي هي تشاكل أبنية. كان ابن الهيثم قد عرف أشعة

الضوء مما مكنه من الكتابة عن ظواهر انتشار الضوء بما فيها ظاهرة تشتته بحيث تتسق مع قوانين الهندسة، وابتكر عددا من التدابير التجريبية لمراجعة صحة النظريات التي كانت مصاغة طبقا لقوانين الهندسة، أي أن هذه التجارب كانت مصممة للتحقق من قوانين علم المناظر الهندسي. تتضح من قراءة أعمال ابن الهيثم حقيقتان هامتان: أولا لم يكن الهدف الوحيد من تصميم تجارب ابن الهيثم هو اختبار بعض الادعاءات الكيفية، بل كان الهدف أيضا الحصول على نتائج كمية. ثانيا كانت الأجهزة والتدابير التي ابتدعها ابن الهيثم متنوعة ومعقدة بالنسبة لزمنها ولم تقتصر على الأجهزة التي استخدمها علماء الفلك.

نجد في علم البصريات الفيزيائي نوعا آخر من العلاقات بين الرياضيات والفيزياء، ولاحقا معنى ثان لكلمة "التجريب". في هذه المرحلة سنجد أن مساهمة الرياضيات هي ذلك التماثل بين الرسومات الهندسية لحركة جسم ثقيل والرسومات الهندسية للانعكاس والانكسار، أي أن الرياضيات أُدخلت في علم البصريات الفيزيائي عن طريق رسومات هندسية ديناميكية تمثل حركة الأجسام الثقيلة التي كان مفترضا أن وصفها الرياضي قد اكتمل. بسبب هذا

التوصيف الرياضي الأولي لمفاهيم نظرية الفيزياء أمكن نقل تلك النظرية إلى المستوى التجريبي، كانت هذه مرحلة مؤقتة لكنها أتاحت مستوى من الوجود لمفاهيم منضبطة إجرائيا وإن كانت معانيها غير محددة بوضوح، مثال ذلك تخطيط ابن الهيثم لحركة المقذوف، الذي استخدمه بعد ذلك كل من كبلر وديكارت.

هناك نوع ثالث من التجريب لم يمارسه ابن الهيثم بنفسه ـ وإن كانت إصلاحاته واكتشافاته في البصريات هي التي سمحت بظهوره ـ نراه في أعمال الفارسي في القرن الثالث عشر. هنا تنحو العلاقة المؤسسة بين الرياضيات والفيزياء نحو بناء نموذج، بحيث يختزل انتشار الضوء داخل وسط طبيعي ـ عن طريق الهندسة ـ إلى انتشاره داخل أداة مصنوعة، مما يعني أننا بصدد تعريف تناظر رياضي تمثيلي بين الطبيعي والأداة المصنوعة؛ مثال ذلك الكرة المملوءة بالماء لتفسير ظاهرة القوس القزح. ووظيفة التجريب هنا هي التعبير عن الشروط الفيزيائية لظاهرة ليس لدينا طريقة أخرى لدراستها مباشرة.

يمكننا إضافة أمثلة أخرى لأنواع التجريب التي ذكرناها، ولكن يكفينا أن نقول إنه برغم اختلاف وظائف هذه الأنواع الثلاثة إلا إنها جميعا آليات ضبط، كما أنها مستويات وجود لمفاهيم إجرائية، لذلك فهي

تختلف جوهريا عن المشاهدة بما في ذلك الرصد الفلكي، ففي كل نوع من الأنواع الثلاثة نجدنا في موقف يقوم فيه العالم ببناء الشيء موضوع الدراسة بنفسه حتى يمكنه أن يتأمله، ومن ثم يحقق في العالم المحسوس فكرة لم تكن ممكنة التحقيق من قبل.

بقيت إصلاحات ابن الهيثم حية بعده، وكذلك ما أرساه من اعتبار التجريب جزءا لا يتجزأ من البرهان في الفيزياء. إن التسلسل الذي يبدأ بابن الهيثم ليصل إلى كبلر وغيره من علماء القرن السابع عشر ثابت، لهذا كانت المعرفة بالعلم العربي ضرورية حتى نتفهم الحداثة الكلاسيكية، إذ تمكننا من فهم كيف أُدخلت المعايير التجريبية في العلم، كما أمكن أن نفهم بشكل أفضل ظهور بعد جديد للتجريب في نهايات القرن السابع عشر وهو "التدقيق".

خاتمة

ختاما نذكر بالنقطتين المركزيتين في هذه المقالة، بداية رأينا أن الإمكانات الجديدة التي أتاحها الجبر كانت منشأ استراتيجية جديدة وعقلانية جديدة. كانت هذه الاستراتيجية نتاجا طبيعيا لتطور الجبر بعد الخوارزمي ولعلاقة الجبر بغيره من فروع الرياضيات، وتمثلت هذه

الاستراتيجية في الكشف الدائم عن مزيد من الأبنية والعمليات في الجبر، والشروع في جدلية التطبيق التي سبق أن أوضحناها في علاقته بالفروع الأخرى. أما العقلانية الجديدة فهي تقوم على الطبيعة الجديدة لمواضيع الرياضيات التي جعلت في الإمكان ما لم يكن ممكنا من قبل، من أمثلة ذلك أن الموضوع الواحد يمكن أن يدرس كهندسة أو كحساب، وأن المسألة يمكن أن يكون لها عدد لا نهائي من الحلول كلها صادقة، وأن يكون الحل الصادق للمسألة هو القول بأنها مسألة يستحيل حلها، وأن نفس الخطوات يمكن تطبيقها على أشياء مختلفة دون الحاجة إلى مزيد من التبرير ... الخ.

شاهدنا كذلك بزوغ مفهوم جديد للبرهان في الفيزياء، وكيف صار المتعارف عليه منذ ذلك الحين أن مستوى وجود الشيء الفيزيائي لم يعد مستوى وجوده "الطبيعي" وإنما نطاق عالم التجريب.

هذه العقلانية الجديدة التي نقول عنها اختصارا أنها جبرية وتجريبية تميز الحداثة الكلاسيكية، وقد أسست في الفترة بين القرن التاسع والقرن الثاني عشر على يد علماء عاشوا في بقاع متباعدة، من أسبانيا المسلمة حتى الصين وكتبوا جميعا باللغة العربية، وقد استحوذ العلماء على تلك العقلانية الجديدة منذ القرن الثاني عشر، ثم ظهرت نسخة

محسنة منها في القرن السادس عشر، لذا يبدو أن المرء إذا أراد أن يفهم حقيقة الحداثة الكلاسيكية فعليه أن يبتعد عن تقسيم الزمن إلى عصور أو حقب بالأسلوب الدارج لدى المؤرخين، فهذه التقسيمات أساسها صلات سببية بين أحداث تاريخ النهضة السياسية والدينية والفنية وبين أحداث العلم، وإنما علينا أن نبحث عن طريق الحقيقة ونترك جانبا الأساطير والخرافات التي حادت بمفكر عظيم كهوسيرل عن الصواب.